ZEFF

Copyright © 2024 by Michael Zeffield

A portion of this book was published under a redacted title, *Being, Not Me-ing*, released October 24, 2022.

ISBN: 978-1-7377443-9-9 (Paperback)
ISBN: 978-1-7377443-8-2 (eBook)

All Rights Reserved. No part of this book may be reproduced or used without written permission of the copyright owner, except in the case of brief quotations embodied in articles and reviews.

Designed & published by Michael Zeffield
Type set in Cochin

For information, please email the writer at:
mtzeff@pm.me

To the Essence,
Of the Essence;
One.

The Aliveness
of every life-form
may be called Being.

The *self*-ness
of every life-form
may be called *Me*.

One may abide as
self-less, thoughtless Being.
Yet, thought
and the movements of *Me*
do not cease.

Being & *Me*-ing
are a sidue coin.

How may one think
while thoughtlessly Being?
How may one Be
while *Me*-ing?

Being & Me-ing

the sideless coin

Thought says:
Do in order to *Be,*
while the Essence
basks as timeless Is-ness.

Being:
The Essence giving rise to
wholeness of action
without effort.

I Am.

There is nowhere to go.
There is nothing to do.

Nowhere is everywhere.
Every *where* is now-here.
Nothing is everything.
Every *thing* is no-thing.

What is,
Is.

All is Here, Now.

Human Being, or
Being human?

The whole gives way
to its parts.

Without air,
who is breathing?
Without Sun,
who is growing?
Without space,
who is living?

Without Being,
who is *Me*-ing?

Action born from *Me*
is inactive.
Action born through *Me*
is the Essence in creation.

Do-ing born from the do-er
does nought.
Do-ing born through the do-er
is the Essence in creation.

A seed does not grow a tree;
the tree grows through the seed.

This is Humility,
surrendered.

Preference and ideality
Are composed of *Me*,
Who chooses, who identifies
One distinction from another.

Is-ness,
Being Is-ness
without distinction,
without dis-integration:

I Am.

Who chooses?
What is chosen?

Identification:
The root of abandonment.

The root of identification:
Attachment to externalities
and concepts of *self*.

Attachment and abandonment,
two facets of one identity:
Me.

Who is *Me?*

Me,
as distinct from *you,*
is upheld by thought.

Without thought,
Me is not.
Without Being,
thought is not.

Does Being
require thought?
Does thought
require *Me?*

Being precedes thought;
thought precedes
the primary distinction:
You and *Me.*

Being Is.

Thought serves *self*
by substantiating it.
In whom *self* appears,
thought runs rampant.

Thought serves Being
by yielding to it.

In whom there is no *whom,*
thought is to Being
as silk is to spider.

What is thought?

Thought begins,
thought ends—
Being Is.

Self begins,
self ends—
Being Is.

The body and the cell:
born within Life,
lived by Life.

Thought and *self*:
born within Being,
lived by Being.

Life, Being:
One.

Direct Awareness
to the masquerades of thought;
the stream of thought
ceases without effort.

Direct Awareness
to the masquerades of *self;*
the stream of *self*
ceases without effort.

When thought is not driven
by thought,
self is foundationless.

Could *Me* appear to be
without the Life
in which *Me* appears to be?

Who thinks — who is thought?
Who eats — who is eaten?

Nourishment and the nourished:
distinct only in appearance.

All belies All:
One whole.

No thing is everything.
Everything is no-thing.

What appears to be seen
is a sensory construction
in the screen of the mind—
not the thing itself.

The thing itself
is not seen;
there is no *thing*
to be seen.

Nobody sees,
and no *thing* is seen—
there is Seeing.

Seeing is Being;
Being is Seeing.

Who am I?

Water flows to the valley—
it does not remain
upon the peak.

Seeds and fertile soil
are carried to the valley
by the rain.

Through the valley
flows the river
from which all Life drinks.

Being is the Water;
the riverbed is *Me*.

This is the landscape
of *self*, surrendered.

Me,
masquerading as I,
is a riverbed
claiming to be Water.

I,
Being *Me,*
is Water
flowing through a riverbed.

Life lives *Me,*
thus the river flows.

Life Is,
I Am.

One, inseparable.

With Awareness
of the masquerades of *Me*,
Integrity is effortless.

Me,
the primary distinction,
surrendered to Being:

Integrity.

The quality
of integral Wholeness.
One.

Me appears to move;
I does not move.

All motion,
all thought,
all action
belies I.

I:
Awareness,
Is-ness,
Being.

Not bound
by the masquerades of *Me*,
who lives?

Silence lives
in the reality:

Nothing to do,
nowhere to go,
no *Me* to be.

Action born of thought
breeds cacophony
amidst silence.

Is-ness,
Being Is-ness:
no-thing and All.

Content in all silence,
silent in all content.

Listening:
the Is-ness
of Life, of Nature.

Here, Now,
the finely-tuned symphony
of harmony resounds.

Who is listening?

Listening,
Aliveness,
Nature:

I Am.

The tree grows
through the seed.
The seed grows
through the tree.

Being Is
the seed,
the seed bearer.

One,
indistinguishable.

Nobody wrote this,
yet words appear
in the screen of the mind.

Nobody shines the Sun,
yet light appears
in the screen of the mind.

Everything Is,
yet the do-er appears
in the screen of the mind.

Who Is?

The I which fruits
from the wilted bloom
of the ephemeral *Me*
is the Is.

I Am.

I Am
simply Being
the Is-ness of All.

The Is-ness of All
simply Being:
I Am.

In the cessation of all *Me*-ing,
the great paradox is revealed:

Being is *Me*-ing.

Being & *Me*-ing:
concepts in words.

All words, all worlds
belie the Essence.

Being has no name.
Being Is.

Here,
Now,
I Am.

Being.
Me-ing.

Now,
what?

The Actor Is.

The Actor
plays the character.

The Actor
is not the character;
the character
is not the Actor.

The Actor
is Being the character.
The character
is Being acted.

Without the Actor,
the character is not.

Without the character,
the Actor is nought.

Who is the character?
Who is the Actor?

Is the Actor
playing the character
while Being the Actor?

Is Being
Me-ing
while Being?

Is the character
absolved in the Actor?
Is *Me*-ing
absolved in Being?

Nothing is gained,
nothing is lost.
All is gained,
all is lost.

As it is,
it Is.

Without a script,
the Actor
makes no mistakes;
the character Is,
as it is.

With a script,
the Actor
makes no mistakes;
the character Is,
as it is.

The Actor Is.
The character Is.

Script or no script,
past or no-past,
future or no-future:

All is improvisation
in the ever-abiding Now.

When the Actor,
playing a character,
meets the Actor
playing a character,
One meets One-*self*.

The Actor Is.
The character Is.

The sideless coin.

Is an instrument
the Music flowing through it?

Is a sound wave
the Music it carries?

Is a musician
the Music being played?

Is Music an instrument?
Is Music a sound wave?
Is Music a musician?

Is Music
without musician,
without sound wave,
without instrument?

Music Is
the sideless coin.

Being
is not a process.
Being Is,
without time.

Me-ing
is a process;
Me-ing is
within time.

Being lives within *Me*.
Me lives within Being.

The timeless lives
within time.
Time lives
within the timeless.

The sideless coin.

Being,
without past,
without future,
makes no mistakes;
Being Is, as it is.

Me,
with memory,
with anticipation,
makes no mistakes;
Me Is, as it is.

Past remembered,
future anticipated:
All is improvisation
in the ever-abiding Now.

It Is, as it is.

Being,
living through *Me*,
is the Actor
playing the character.

Being,
living through *Me*,
is Music
playing the musician.

Being, *Me*-ing;
Music, musician;
Actor, character:
One and the same.

The sideless coin.

Can *Me* live
without Being?

Can Being live
without *Me*-ing?

Is Being
not *Me*-ing?

Is *Me*
not Being?

Being &
Me-ing:

The sideless coin.

Being is born *Me*-ing.
Me is Being, born.

Being & *Me*-ing
bear the same birth,
and die the same death.

Yet,
the death of *Me*
is not the death of Being.

Without Being,
Me is not.
Without *Me*,
Being is not.

Being & *Me*-ing:
The sideless coin.

Cosmos and *Chaos:*
order and disorder.

Preserving cosmos,
or abating cosmos,
is chaos.

Mitigating chaos,
or maintaining chaos,
is chaos.

Yet,
preserving,
abating,
mitigating,
maintaining,
is cosmos.

Chaos Is.
Cosmos Is.

The sideless coin.

Me is the knower
and the known.

Yet,
Me knows not *Me*.

Me is the seer
and the seen.

Yet,
Me sees not *Me*.

Who knows?
Who sees?
What is known?
What is seen?

Being knows not;
Being is not known.

Being sees not;
Being is not seen.

Being Is.

Yet,
the knower,
the known,
the seer,
and the seen,
are Being.

The sideless coin.

Being is writing words
through the mind
of *Me*.

Being is reading words
through the eyes
of *Me*.

Being is alive
as *Me*.

Here, Now.

Be,
as *Me*.

It Is,
as it is.

I Am,
as I am.

Being & *Me*-ing:
the sideless coin.

www.ingramcontent.com/pod-product-compliance
Lightning Source LLC
Chambersburg PA
CBHW011522070526
44585CB00022B/2504